ACTIVITY 1

# Spring Scene Photograph Matching

1. Cut out the images.

2. Present your child with two sets of 12 cards. One of the sets contains square photographs. The second set of cards contains circles with a small section of these photographs.

3. Your child can match the square photographs with the circles.

# CUT OUT

# CUT OUT

# CUT OUT

# CUT OUT

ACTIVITY 2

# Ranking Spring Colors

1. On the next page you'll find three color palettes. Cut out each of the rectangles.

2. Present your child with the five colors that belong to one color palette.

3. Ask your child to grade the colors from darkest to lightest shade.

# CUT OUT

ACTIVITY 3

1. Cut out the images.

2. Present your child with two sets of 8 cards. One set contains photographs. The other set contains isolated objects that match the scenes on the photographs.

3. Your child can match one card in the set to a card from the other set.

# CUT OUT

# CUT OUT

# CUT OUT

# CUT OUT

ACTIVITY 4

# Beginning Sounds

Draw a line to match the beginning sound of the image on the left to a letter on the right.

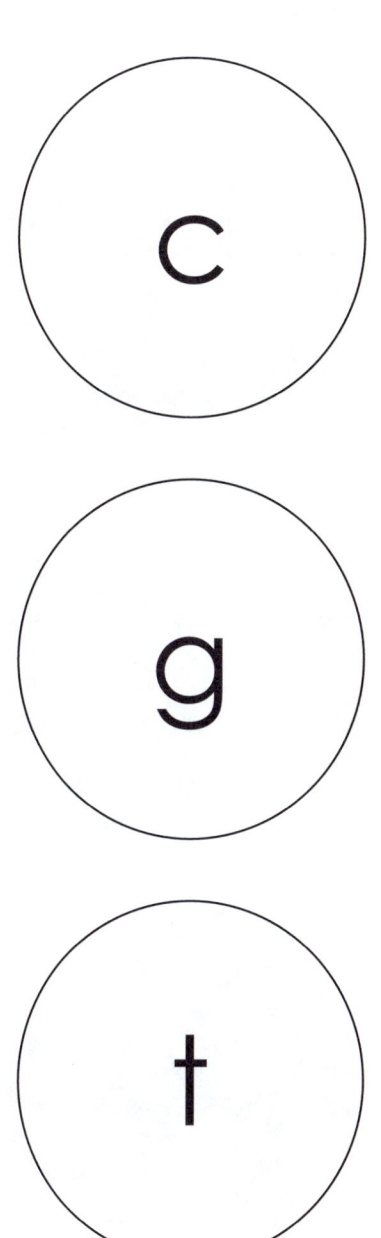

ACTIVITY 4

# Beginning Sounds

Draw a line to match the beginning sound of the image on the left to a letter on the right.

ACTIVITY 4

# Beginning Sounds

Draw a line to match the beginning sound of the image on the left to a letter on the right.

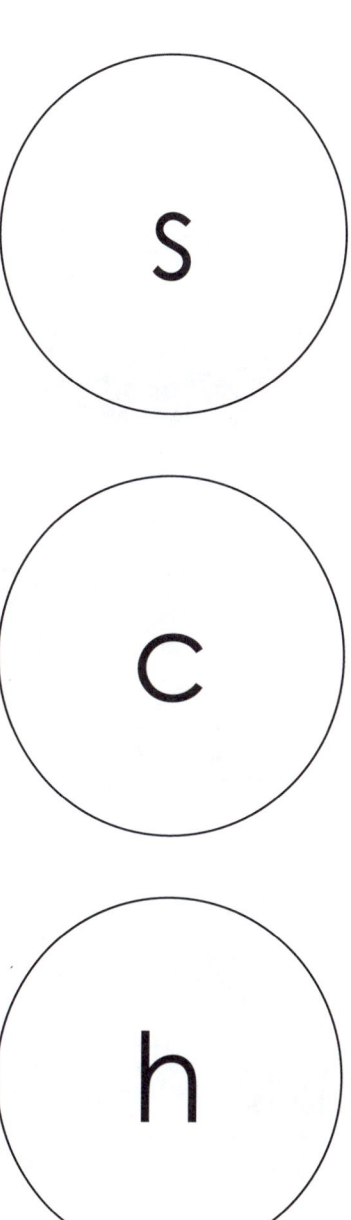

ACTIVITY 4

# Beginning Sounds

Draw a line to match the beginning sound of the image on the left to a letter on the right.

# ACTIVITY 4

# Beginning Sounds

Draw a line to match the beginning sound of the image on the left to a letter on the right.

ACTIVITY 4

# Beginning Sounds

Draw a line to match the beginning sound of the image on the left to a letter on the right.

w

l

d

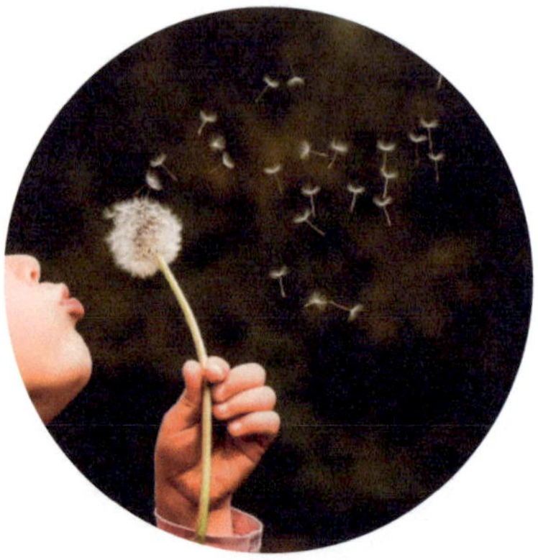

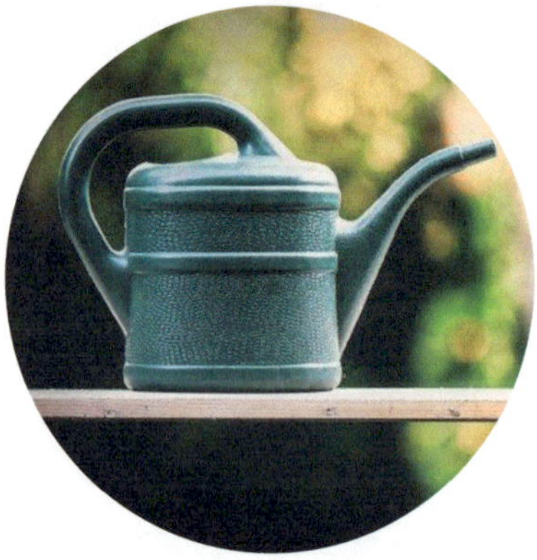

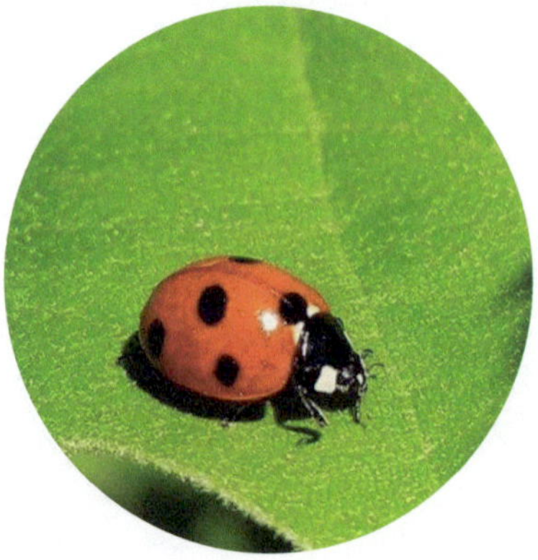

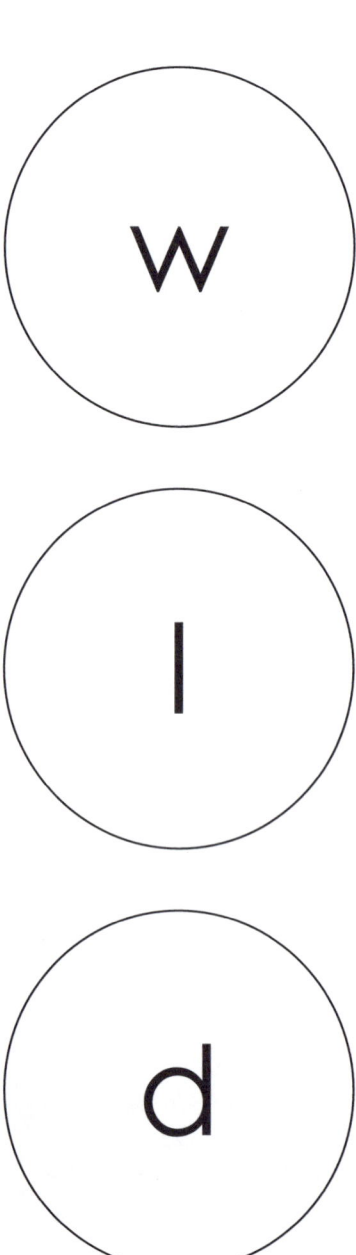

# ACTIVITY 4

# Beginning Sounds

Draw a line to match the beginning sound of the image on the left to a letter on the right.

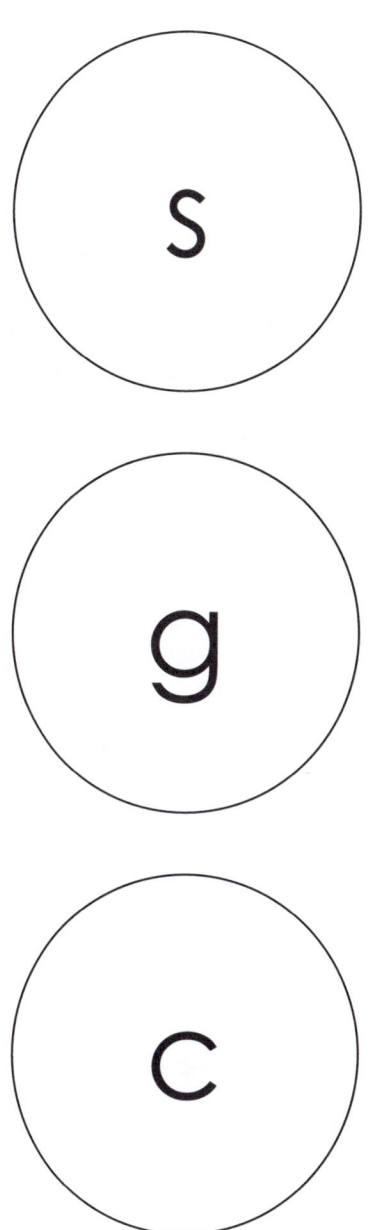

ACTIVITY 5

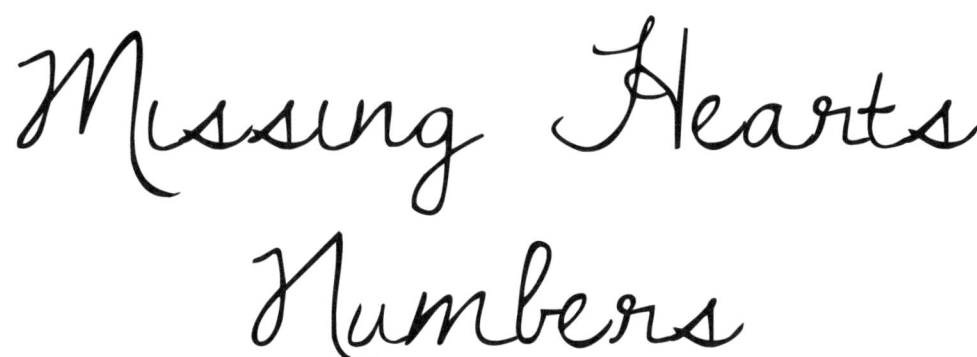

1. Cut out the images.

2. Put out five rows of numbers and five separate hearts that match.

3. Your child can match the hearts to the missing numbers in the row.

4. Since all of the numbers will be used up, there is a built-in control of error.

CUT OUT

CUT OUT

CUT OUT

CUT OUT

CUT OUT

13
12
10

15
14
13

CUT OUT

CUT OUT

CUT OUT

ACTIVITY 6

# Floral Pinprick

Use a large pushpin to punch holes in the grey dots around the image. The goal is to cut the shape out of the paper without scissors. It's helpful to put the paper on some cork and pin it down at the corners to keep it in place.

ACTIVITY 7

1. Cut out the cards.

2. Your child can line up the cards in the correct order of the life cycle.

3. Optional: if you have a miniature version of a caterpillar/butterfly or a stuffed animal, place this with the cards as well to bring the activity to life.

CUT OUT

egg

caterpillar

chrysalis (pupa)

butterfly

ACTIVITY 8

1. Cut out the three strips.

2. Your child can practice cutting along the dotted line to the illustration.

# CUT OUT

# ACTIVITY 9

# Egg Lacing Card

1. Cut out the easter egg.

2. Use a hole punch to create holes along the outline of the shape, about an inch apart.

3. Your child can lace the shape using a shoelace or a blunt needle with some yarn.

ACTIVITY 10

# Egg Counting

1. Cut out the number cards.

2. You can use the paper eggs that are included, but it's even more fun to use 10 actual (cooked / fake) eggs in a basket instead, if you happen to have them.

3. Grab an empty egg carton or use the printed image of the egg carton instead.

4. Place the number cards in random order face down in a pile. Gather your basket of eggs. Place the carton next to it.

5. Your child can draw a number card, count out the correct number of eggs and place them in the egg carton.

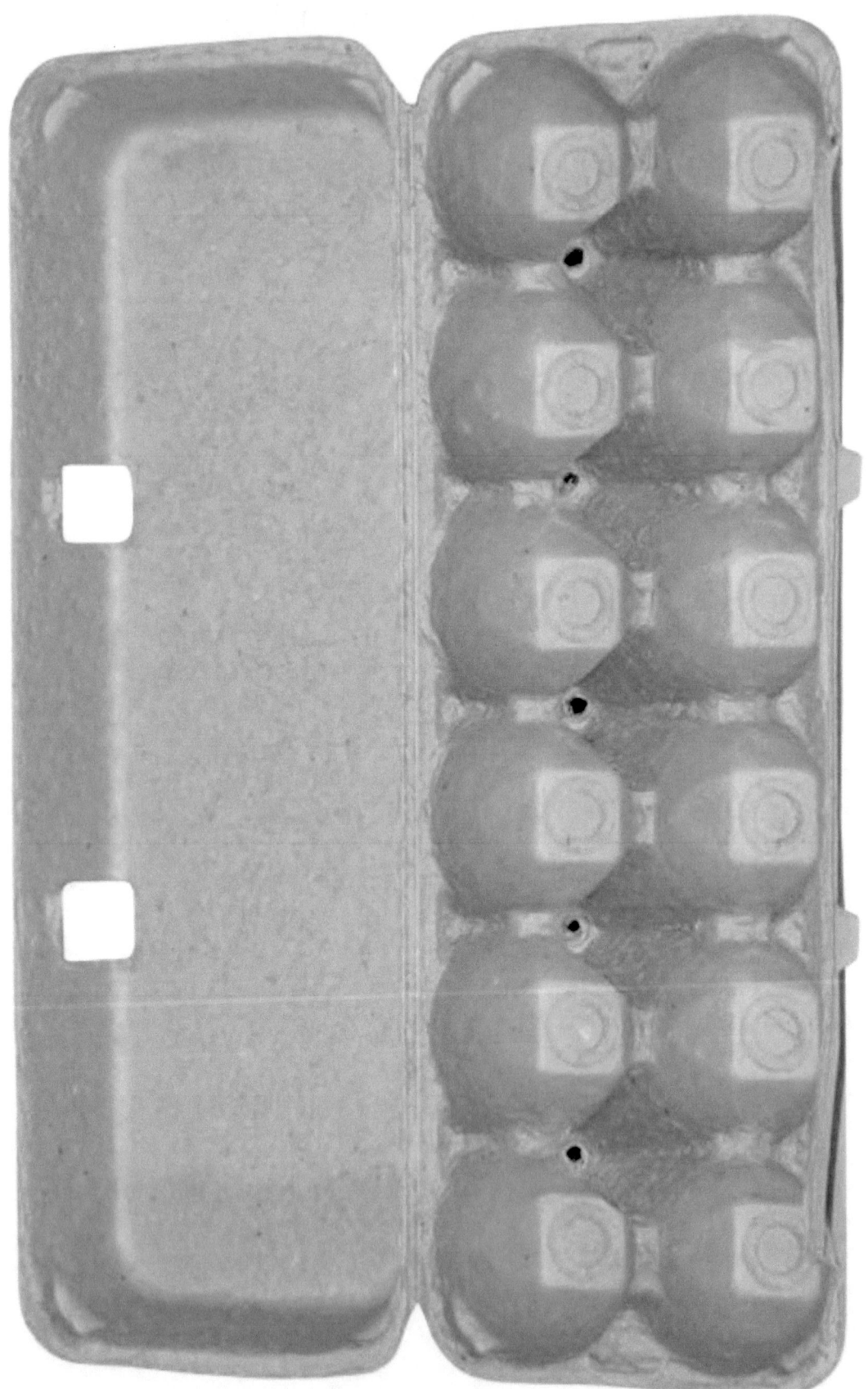

CUT OUT

| 1 | 2 | 3 |
| 4 | 5 | 6 |
| 7 | 8 | 9 |
| 10 | | |

CUT OUT

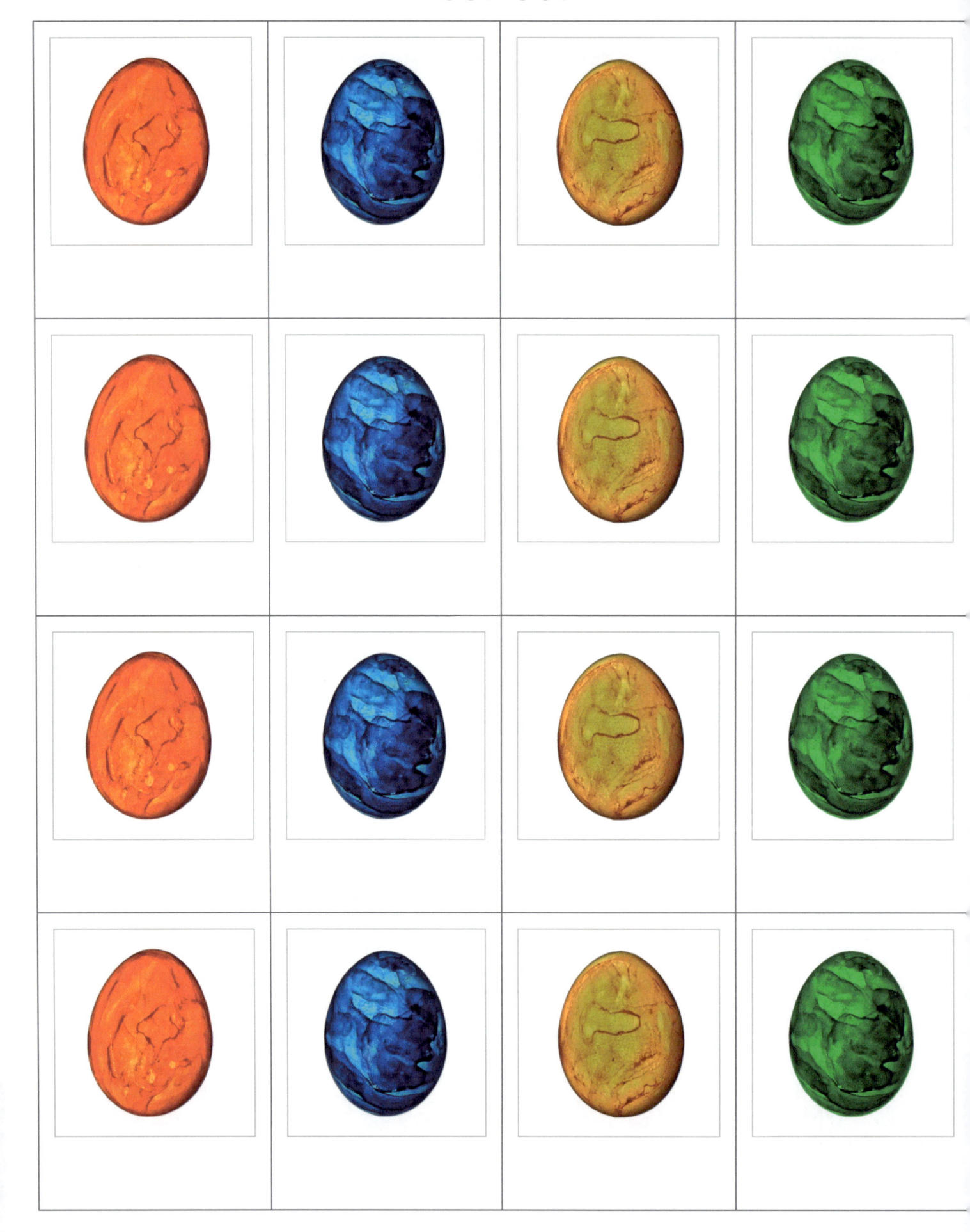

# ACTIVITY 11

# Rhyming Riddles

1. Cut out the picture and riddle cards.

2. Present the picture cards to your child. Make sure it's clear to him or her what is displayed.

3. Read the riddle aloud to your child. Ask him or her to match it to a picture card.

CUT OUT

I rhyme with "lipstick".

I am a _____ (picnic).

I rhyme with "habit".

I am a _____ (rabbit).

CUT OUT

CUT OUT

I rhyme with "brick".

I am a _____ (chick).

I rhyme with "jam".

I am a _____ (lamb).

CUT OUT

CUT OUT

I rhyme with "apple pie".

I am a _____ (butterfly).

I rhyme with "leg".

I am an _____ (egg).

CUT OUT

I rhyme with "nail".

I am a _____ (snail).

I rhyme with "tree".

I am a _____ (bee).

# ACTIVITY 12

## Spring Pattern Strips

1. Cut out the eight strips and the eight separate cards.

2. Present all of the material to your child. Or, to make it easier at first, just take four strips and four (matching) separate cards.

3. Your child can find the image that's supposed to come next on a strip based on the sequencing of the images.

4. Once the work is complete, all of the separate cards should have been matched, creating a built-in control of error.

CUT OUT

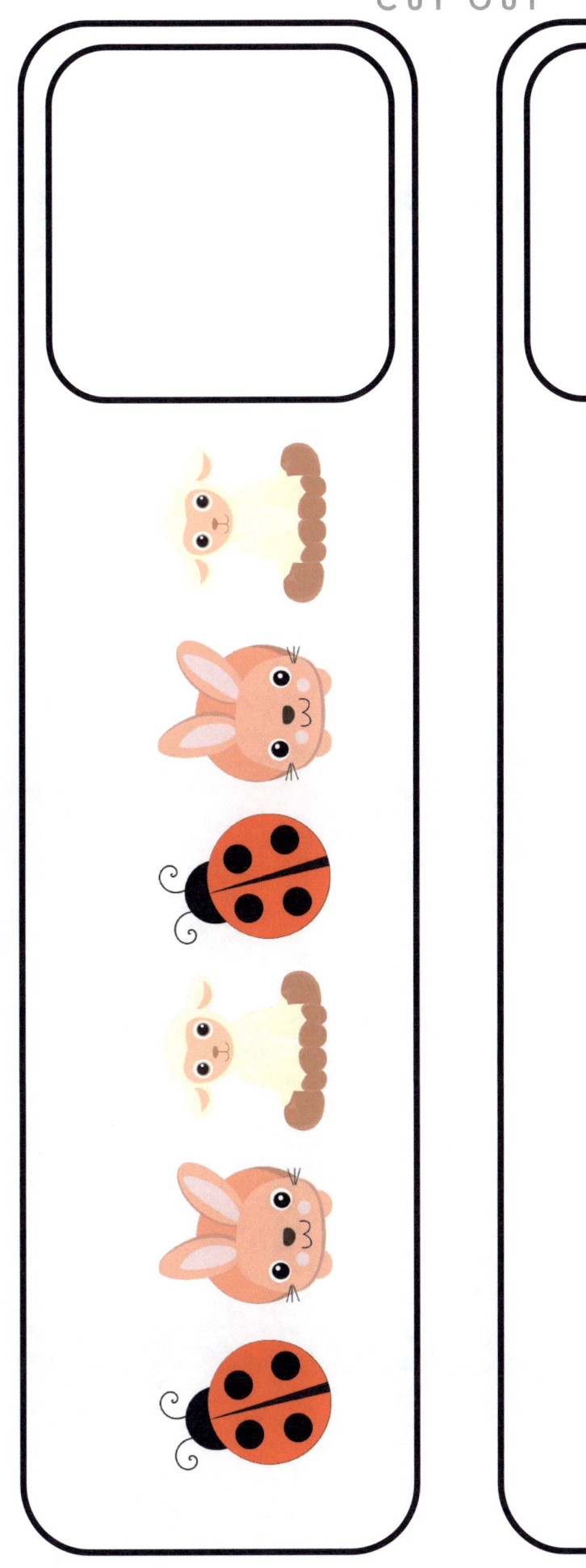

CUT OUT

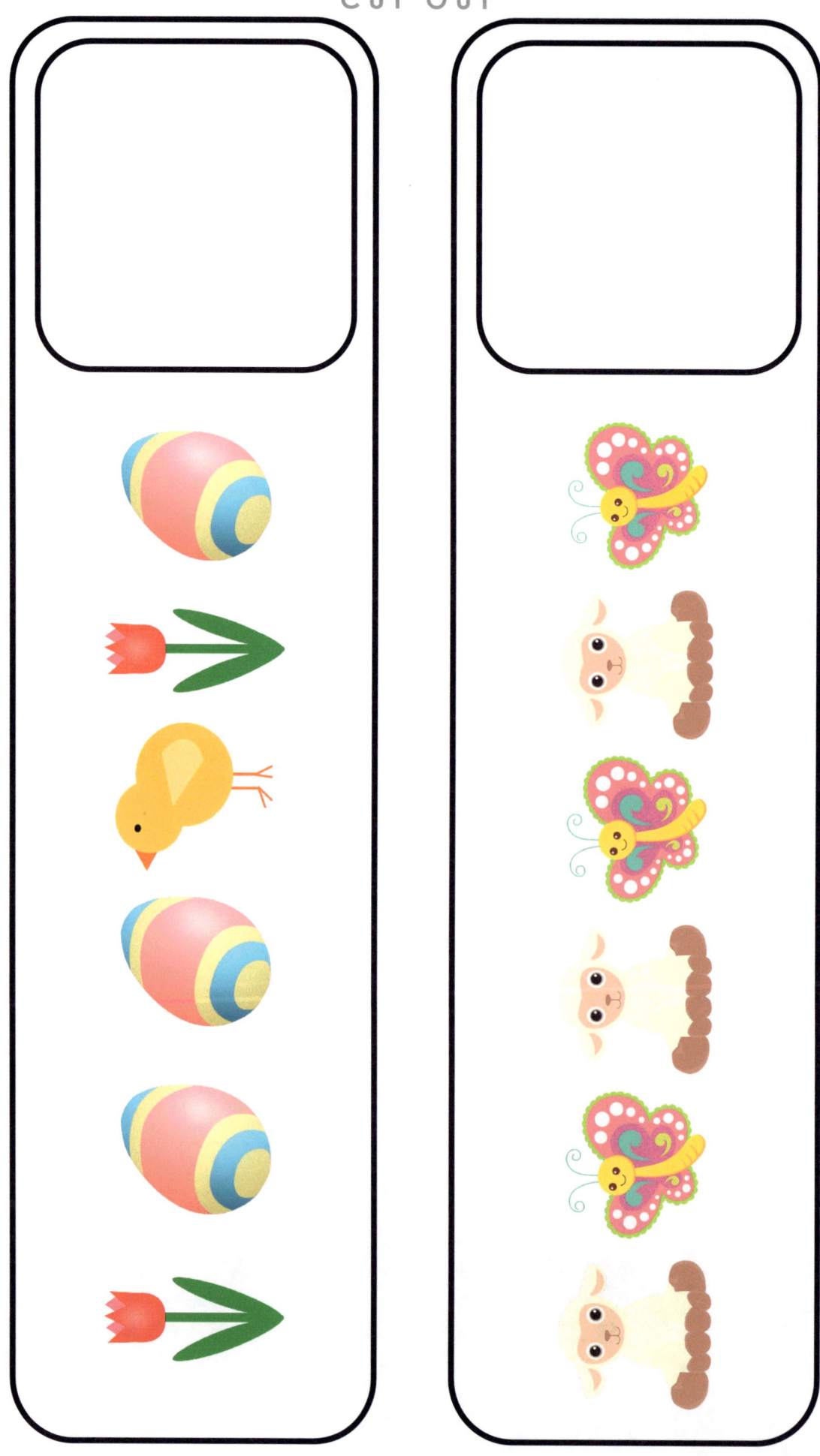

CUT OUT

CUT OUT

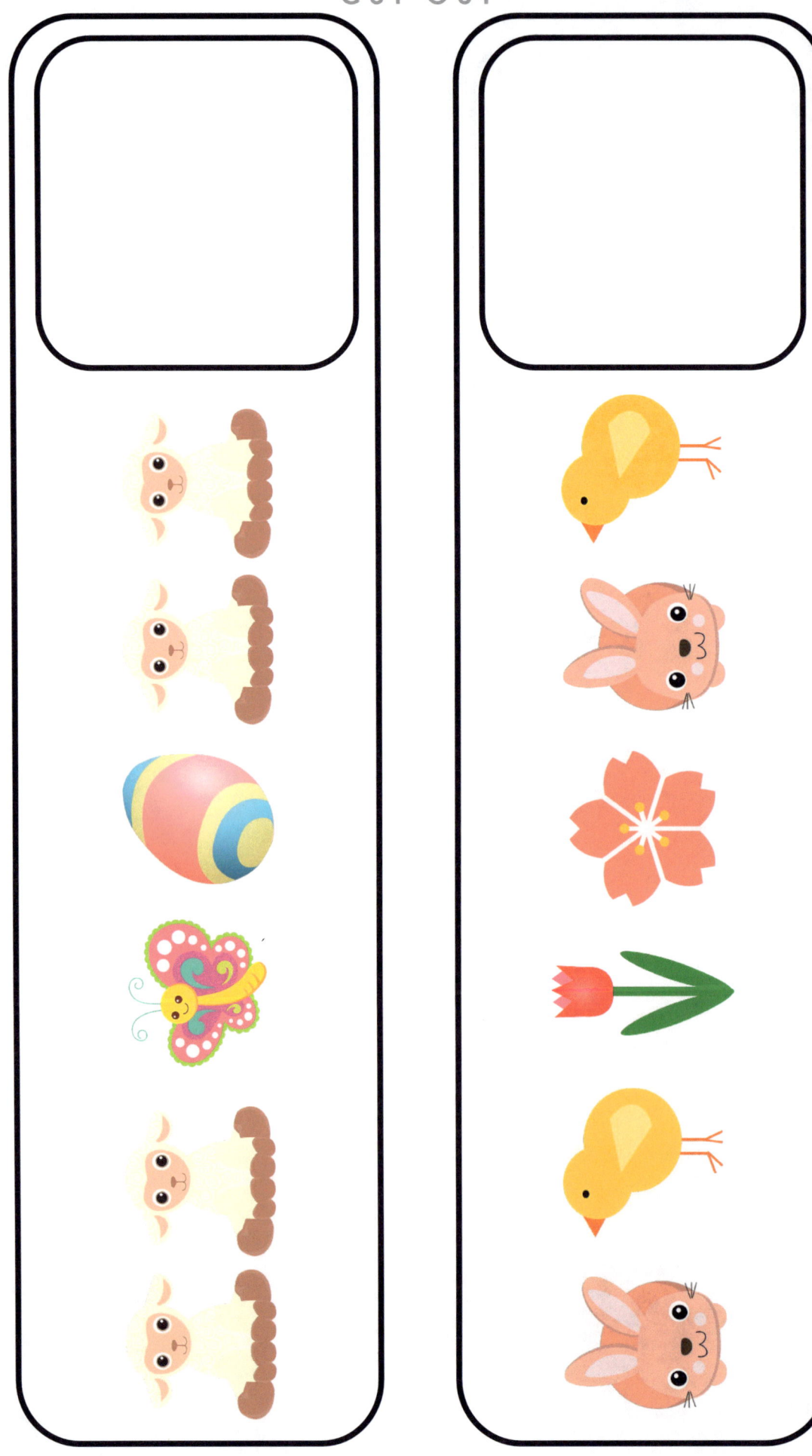

CUT OUT

ACTIVITY 13

# Spring Plant or Animal?

1. Cut out the cards.

2. Lay out the cover cards with the text "plant" and "animal". Put the picture cards in a little basket next to it.

3. Your child can determine for each card whether a plant or an animal is pictured and put it next to the cover card.

CUT OUT

| plant | animal |

CUT OUT

plant or animal?

plant or animal?

plant or animal?

plant or animal?

CUT OUT

plant or animal?

plant or animal?

plant or animal?

plant or animal?

CUT OUT

plant or animal?

plant or animal?

plant or animal?

plant or animal?

CUT OUT

plant or animal?

plant or animal?

plant or animal?

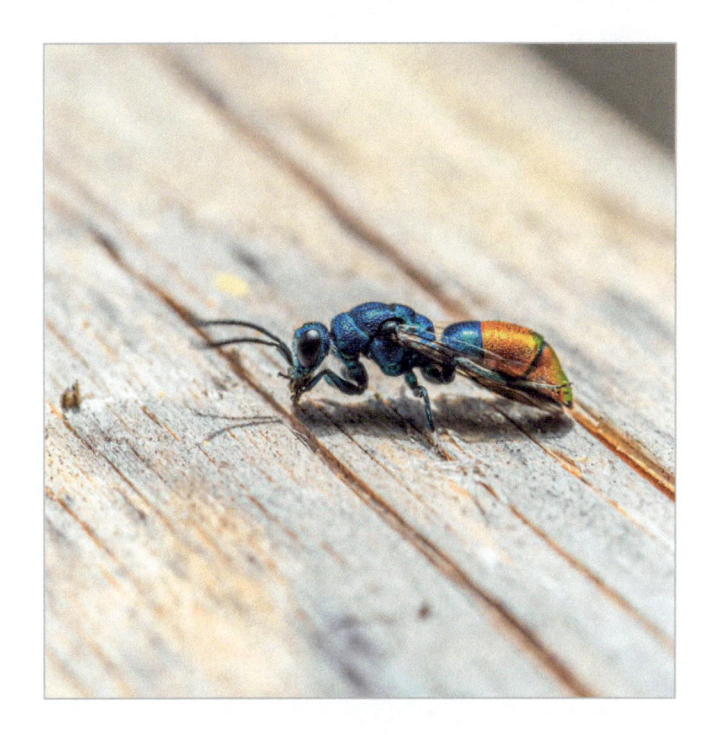

plant or animal?

CUT OUT

plant or animal?

plant or animal?

plant or animal?

plant or animal?

ACTIVITY 14

# Spring Living or Non-living?

1. Cut out the cards.

2. Lay out the cover cards with the text "living" and "non-living". Put the picture cards in a little basket next to it.

3. Your child can determine for each card whether a living or a non-living thing is pictured and put it next to the cover card.

CUT OUT

| living | non-living |

CUT OUT

living or non-living?

living or non-living?

living or non-living?

living or non-living?

CUT OUT

living or non-living?

living or non-living?

living or non-living?

living or non-living?

CUT OUT

living or non-living?

living or non-living?

living or non-living?

living or non-living?

CUT OUT

living or non-living?

living or non-living?

living or non-living?

living or non-living?

CUT OUT

living or non-living?

living or non-living?

living or non-living?

living or non-living?

# ACTIVITY 15

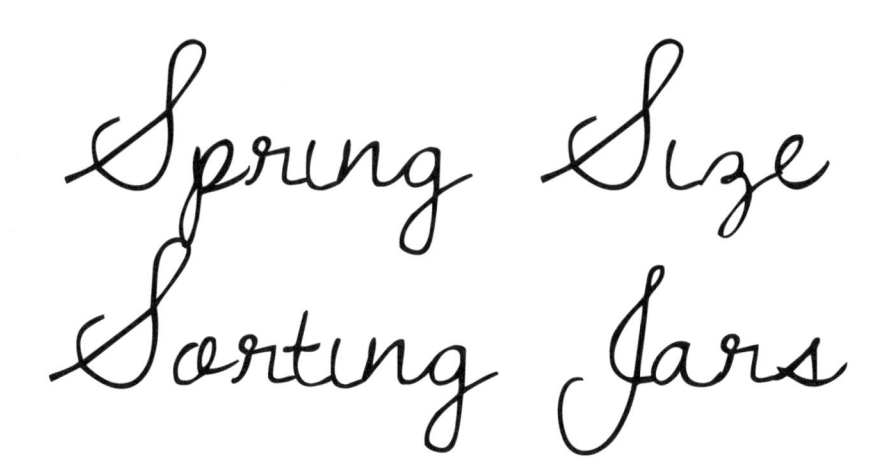

# Spring Size Sorting Jars

1. Cut out the heart, rose and balloon circles. No need to cut out the jars.

2. Your child can sort the images: the big ones go into the big jar and the small ones go into the small jar.

3. You could present all of the images at once, or you could only lay out only one of the shapes first, depending on what challenge suits your child's age.

big

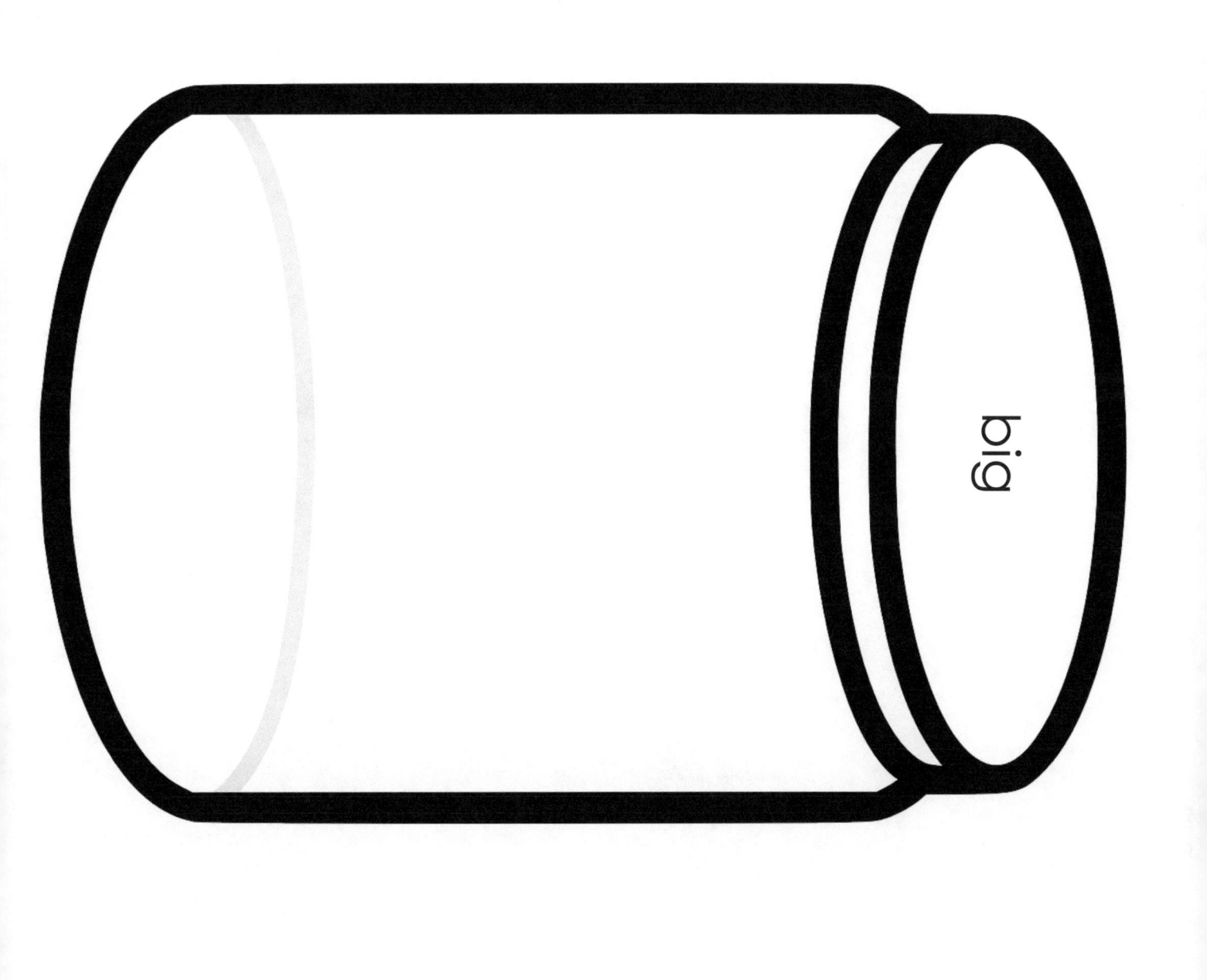

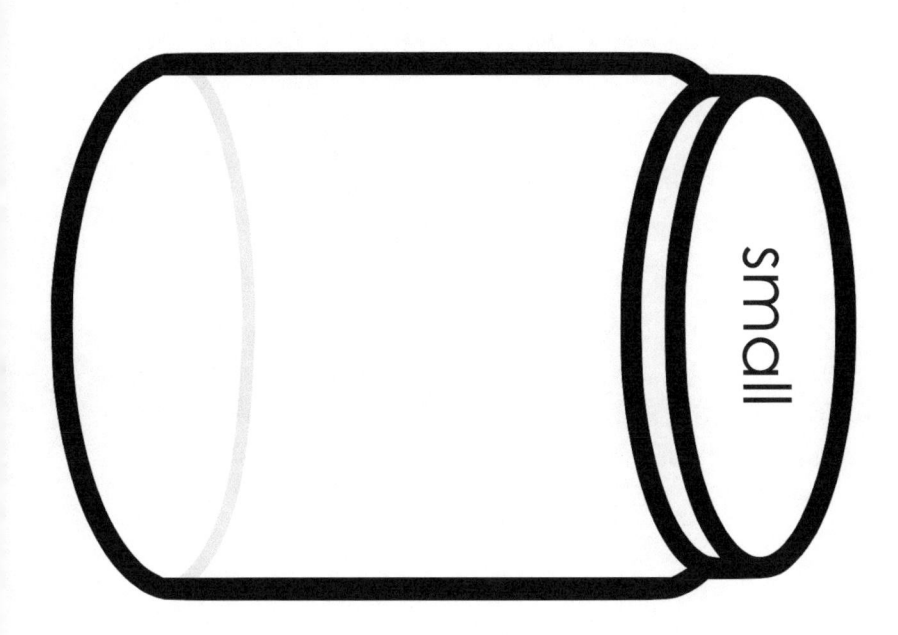

small

CUT OUT

CUT OUT

CUT OUT

ACTIVITY 16

# Spring or Autumn?

Draw a line to match each picture to the season it belongs to: spring or autumn?

spring

autumn

ACTIVITY 16

# Spring or Autumn?

Draw a line to match each picture to the season it belongs to: spring or autumn?

spring

autumn

# ACTIVITY 17

# Spring Counting

How many can you count?

____  ____  ____

# ACTIVITY 17

## Spring Counting

How many can you count?

_____     _____     _____

# ACTIVITY 17

## Spring Counting

How many can you count?

# ACTIVITY 18

# Spring Silhouettes

Draw a line to match the animal on the left to its silhouette on the right.

# ACTIVITY 19

# Butterfly Labyrinth

Draw a line to let the butterfly fly to the flower. Try not to fly into the edges!

ACTIVITY 20

# Farm or wild animal?

1. Cut out the cards.

2. Lay out the cover cards with the text "farm animal" and "wild animal". Put the picture cards in a little basket next to it.

3. Your child can determine for each card whether the animal is typically one who lives on a farm or in the wild and put it next to the cover card.

CUT OUT

# farm animal

farm or wild animal?

farm or wild animal?

farm or wild animal?

CUT OUT

farm or wild animal?

farm or wild animal?

farm or wild animal?

CUT OUT

# wild animal

farm or wild animal?

farm or wild animal?

farm or wild animal?

CUT OUT

farm or wild animal?

farm or wild animal?

farm or wild animal?

# ACTIVITY 21

# Spring Subtraction

How many pictures remain?

3 - 1 = \_\_\_\_

4 - 2 = \_\_\_\_

3 - 2 = \_\_\_\_

5 - 3 = \_\_\_\_

ACTIVITY 21

# Spring Subtraction

How many pictures remain?

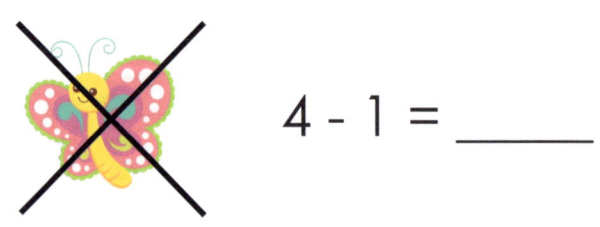

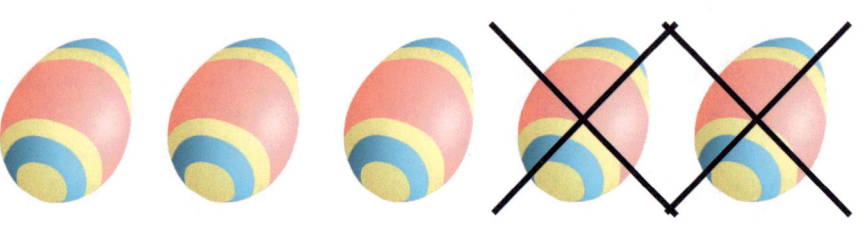

2 - 1 = \_\_\_\_

4 - 2 = \_\_\_\_

4 - 1 = \_\_\_\_

5 - 2 = \_\_\_\_

ACTIVITY 22

# Spring Item Color Matching

1. Cut out the color cards and the picture circles.

2. Your child can sort the pictures by color and put them next to the color cards. You can present your child with as many pictures as you feel are the right challenge.

CUT OUT

red

green

yellow

blue

CUT OUT

# ACTIVITY 23
## Spring Halves

Draw a line to match the animal on the left to its silhouette on the right.

ACTIVITY 24

# Let's Make 10

Draw more to make 10. Finish the addition equation.

8 + _____ = 10

6 + _____ = 10

ACTIVITY 24

# Let's Make 10

Draw more to make 10. Finish the addition equation.

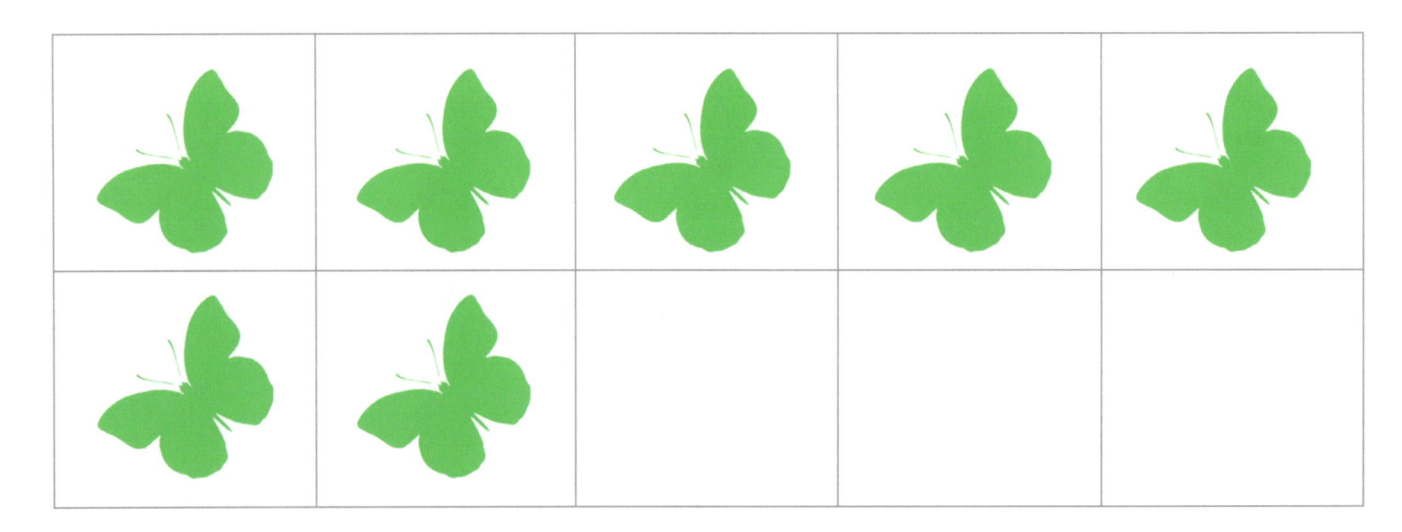

7 + _____ = 10

4 + _____ = 10

ACTIVITY 24

# Let's Make 10

Draw more to make 10. Finish the addition equation.

3 + _____ = 10

9 + _____ = 10

# ACTIVITY 25

# Spring Pattern Matching

1. Cut out the images.

2. For each of the illustrations there are nine cards with three different patterns.

3. Present your child with the nine cards of one illustration.

4. Ask your child to find the matching patterns (instead of the matching colors).

CUT OUT

CUT OUT

CUT OUT

CUT OUT

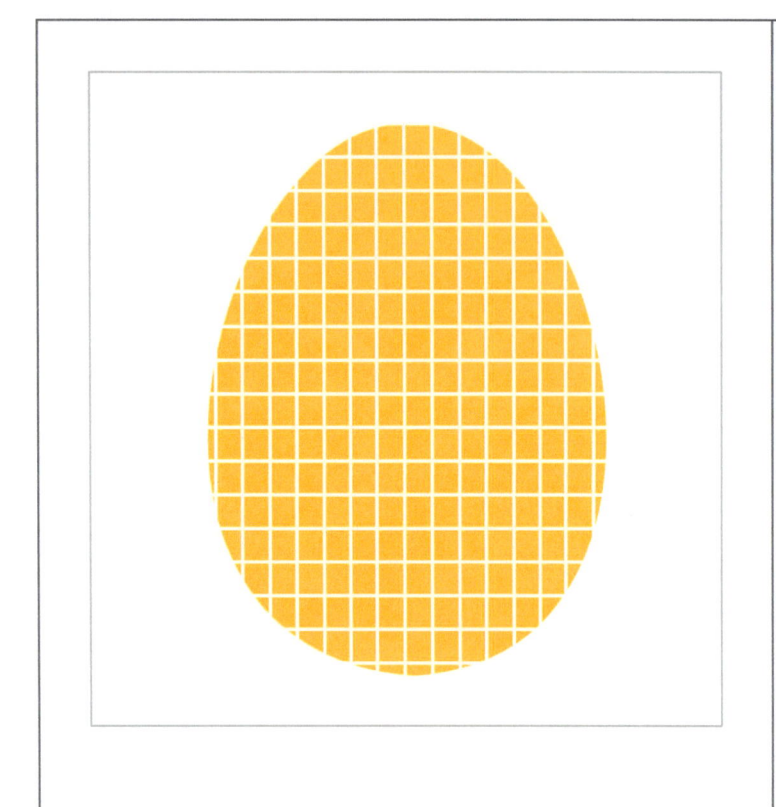

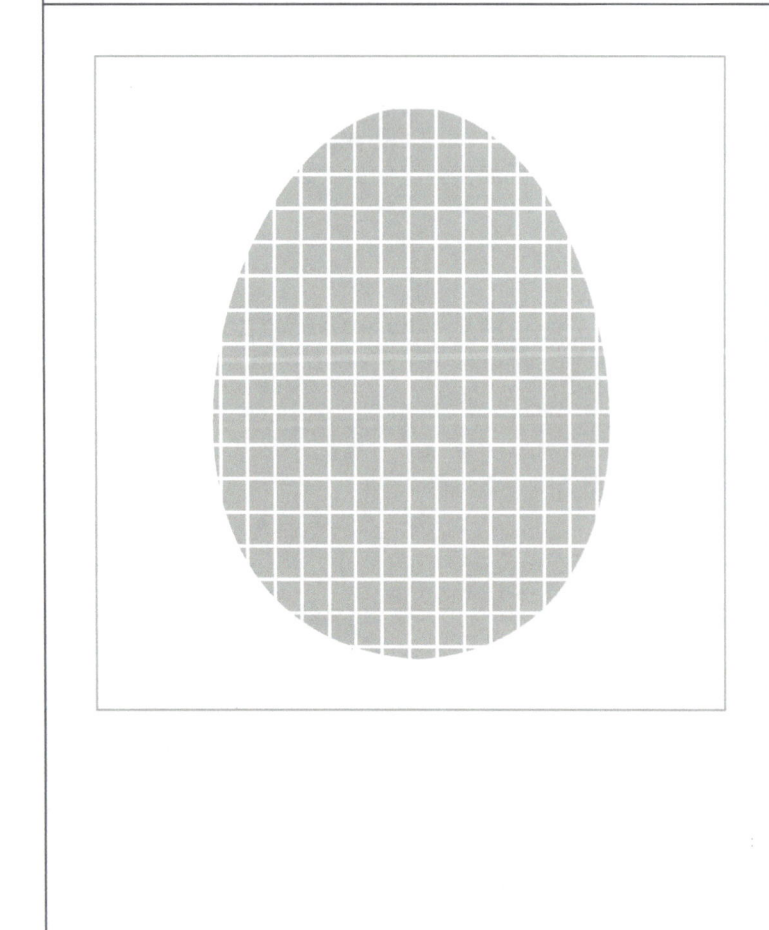

CUT OUT

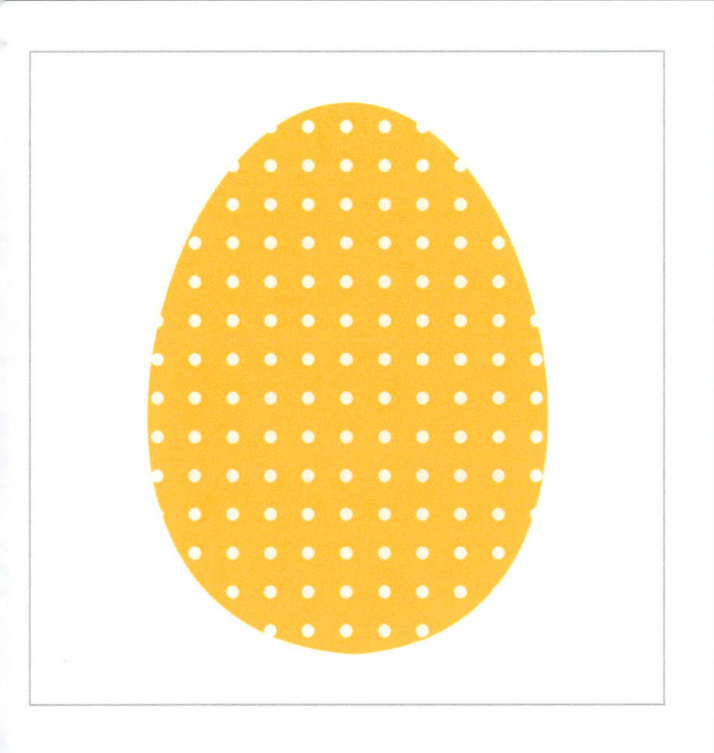

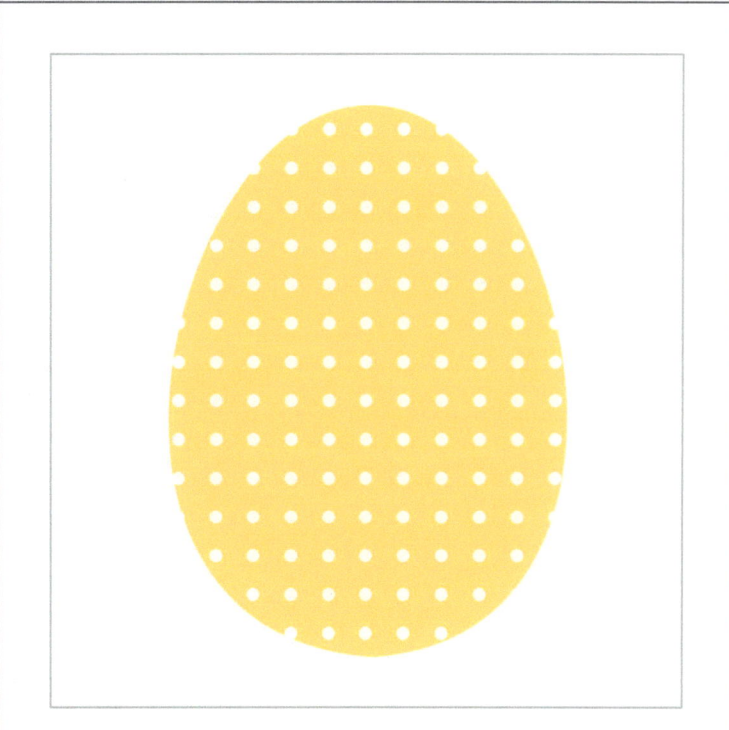

CUT OUT

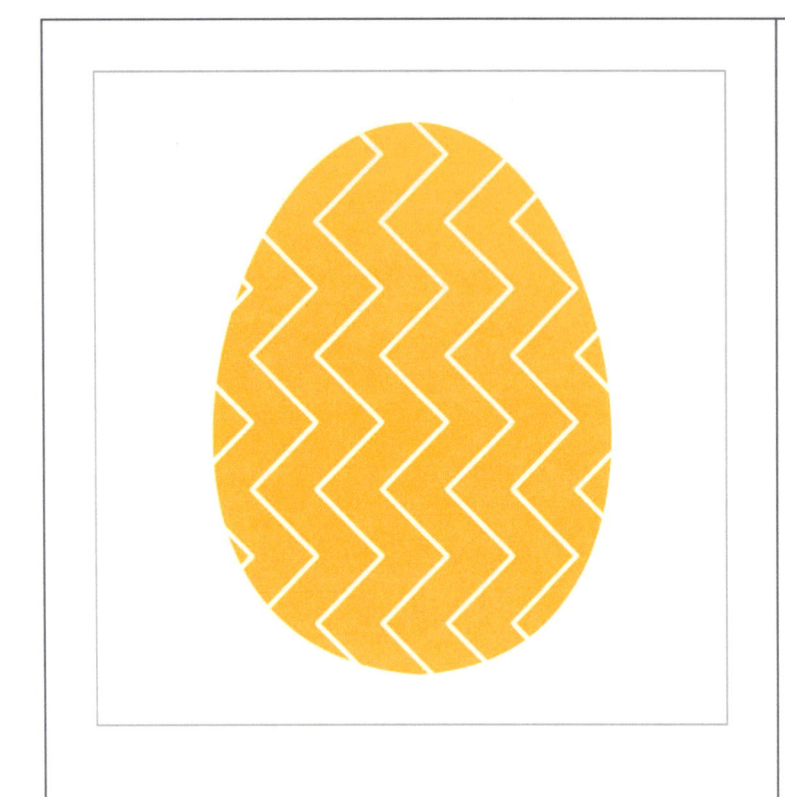

CUT OUT

CUT OUT

CUT OUT

Made in United States
Troutdale, OR
03/24/2025